Contents

GOLF. THE LADIES TEE.

INDEX TO FEATURED COURSES

GOLF

·ON OLD PICTURE POSTCARDS·

Tom Serpell

Ladies Pavilion, Bulwell Golf Links, Nottingham. "Clumber" series postcard no. 157, published by
A. Hindley of Nottingham.

Designed and Published by
Reflections of a Bygone Age
Keyworth, Nottingham.

Printed by Adlard Print and Typesetting Services,
Ruddington, Notts.

© **Tom Serpell, September 1988**

ISBN 0 946245 21 5

 Tom Serpell was born in Tavistock in 1948. After school in
Kent, then Eastbourne, he went to Exeter College, Oxford,
graduating in "Greats" in 1969. He is now general manager of
Odin Developments Ltd, a new packaging company; his office
is in Stevenage.

He, his wife and three daughters live near Cambridge. Tom
is a member of Royston Golf Club.

His collections of golfing books and postcards have been ac-
quired over some twenty years by him and his father, Sir David
Serpell, who lives in Dartmouth.

INTRODUCTION

The era of Nicklaus, Watson, Ballesteros, Faldo and Woosnam may seem to be golf's heyday. Their feats of low scoring, prodigious driving and vast earnings are brought to us as they occur across huge distances in full colour on our televisions, with expert and researched commentary from past luminaries of the game. Today's views of tonsured courses in exotic places make golf of past decades seem colourless; a pale forerunner of the game we have today.

But consider if you will what talent it must have taken to devise the courses by which these great players of today may still be humbled more than a century after their first use; what skills the players of those days must have had to play them with equipment unblessed by modern technology.

There was an earlier heyday for golf. Around the turn of this century a number of factors came together to create a boom in this game which was in its context every bit as significant as today's.

Although golf had been played in Scotland at least as early as the 15th century, until the mid-19th century it had been a game of few participants; another sport of kings indeed, for we know that the Stuart Kings of Scotland played. But the second half of Victoria's reign saw the foundation of an ever-growing number of clubs and courses, initially in Scotland, then in England, then overseas.

The railways had made distant parts of Britain accessible to city-dwellers, who, having discovered the combined attractions of scenery, fresh air and golf, flocked to resorts embellished with newly-founded clubs.

The newspapers carried stories of the feats of sportsmen, professional and amateur, on whom the new golfing public could aspire to model themselves.

And not least the picture postcard was itself in its pomp. Millions of cards a year were sent to keep families and friends abreast of travellers' news. It was natural that cards should depict the places and attractions which had lured their senders away from home, and act as further advertisement to others to take up golf. Many people indeed collected the cards they received. Postcard collecting, like golf, is now enjoying a new heyday. This book aims to illustrate the first combined golden age of golf and picture postcards, and to remind today's players of the foundations on which golf in the late 20th century is built. It is based on postcards collected by my father, David Serpell, and myself over nearly twenty years, and researched from our own golf library. In this respect it may not be perfectly representative of the postcard population, nor of golf at that time. However, insofar as any anthology must intrinsically be personal, this one has the merit of being especially so. I hope that it both entertains and informs, by including postcards from as many different places of interest as possible.

I should like to thank Jane Somers Cocks for lending illustration 195 of Chagford golf course; Barbara Saul for ruining her weekends typing my drafts; my wife Vivienne for being a patient "golf-postcard widow"; and the fellow-collector without whom none of this would have been possible, my father, David Serpell.

Tom Serpell, August 1988

One of a set of sporting vicars by Scottish artist Cynicus, published by his own company

Golfing Postcards

It will readily be apparent from the variety of illustrations in this volume that golf was an attractive subject from the viewpoint of postcard publishers. In the Edwardian era, when picture postcards were at the height of their popularity, and millions went through the postal system daily, both photographic and artist-drawn scenes of courses went on sale for sportsmen and women, locals and tourists to buy and send.

Well-known comic artists like Tom Browne and Donald McGill used golfing situations as the basis of postcard cartoons. The trend continued even after the First World War when the picture postcard generally became less used as the telephone took over some of its functions. Thus many of the illustrations in this book are post-1918, though generally the cards of the inter-war period were of inferior quality to their Edwardian predecessors.

Golf postcards are today extremely popular and widely-collected. The rarest examples are those featuring famous players, but cards of courses usually cost from £2-4 each, and comic cards normally rate a price in excess of £3. The best scenic examples are those on photographic cards with close-ups of golfers in action, but artist-drawn cards are also sought-after.

For more details on the various postcard publishers, see page 59.

Useful postcard reading for the beginner:

IPM Postcard Catalogue *(International Postcard Market, P.O. Box 190, Lewes, East Sussex)*
RF Postcard Catalogue *(RF Postcards, 17 Hilary Crescent, Rayleigh, Essex)*
Postcard Collecting — a beginners' guide *(Reflections of a Bygone Age)*
Picture Postcard Monthly *(Reflections of a Bygone Age)*
Picture Postcard Annual *(Reflections of a Bygone Age)*

'Golf is not the only game on earth' (C. Dana Gibson postcard sketch — see also illus. 221-3)

Cynicus comic

Cynicus comic.

LINKS

The very first golf courses, of perhaps only four or five holes, were laid out among coastal sand dunes known as "linksland": which lies between the shore and cultivable land. This terrain lent itself to the hitting of a small ball because it was naturally seeded by grasses and low-growing plants but hostile to lush vegetation or trees. It was often populated by huge numbers of rabbits which grazed the sheltered gullies into natural fairways and greens.

As golf has grown in popularity many new kinds of terrain have been developed for golf courses, but links golf, the original game, has unique charms and difficulties which to many make it the best of all. The Open is still only played on links courses.

Many links courses seem to the untutored eye to be innocuous: smooth and treeless. But not only are they subtle and prone to unpredictable bounces, they are open to the sea "breezes" which can render short par-fours into full 3-shotters.

1. Saunton. This photographic panorama of Braunton Burrows in North Devon, published locally by R.L. Knight, shows the true linksland to perfection. Among the towering dunes covered with marram and other self-sown grasses and flora lies Saunton Golf Club.

2. Saunton Golf Club. Postcard by Chapman & Son, Dawlish, 1935. Founded in 1918, with a second course opening in 1935, the whole was turned into a training ground for U.S. troops in World War 2. It was reopened in 1951 with layout by C.K. Cotton.

3. Westward Ho! Across the Torridge estuary from Saunton lies a unique triangular spit of linksland bordered on one side by a Pebble Ridge which protects the oldest extant golf course in England, Westward Ho!, home of the Royal North Devon Golf Club. Founded in 1864, 8 years after the earliest recorded play there, it produced two of England's greatest golfers: the amateur Horace Hutchinson and 5-times Open Champion J.H. Taylor. Taylor started as a caddie at the club and was its President when he died. Pictorial Stationery Co. postcard, sent from Westward Ho! in August 1906. It features the eleventh hole, and the course's unique hazard, the Great Sea Rush, described by the sender *"... these grow to 7ft. high and have very sharp points"*. They have been known to pierce a golf ball!

(more hazards on pages 30-31)

4. Lelant. West Cornwall Golf Club was laid out here in 1889. British and U.S. Open Champion Jim Barnes began his golf career here as a caddie. Argall & Co's series, posted at Lelant on Christmas Eve 1909.

5. St Enodoc. An inter-war photographic card of one of the most enjoyable of links. Not long, but with high dunes and lovely turf, St Enodoc lies between Rock and Polzeath in North Cornwall. Famous both for its 60ft. bunker known as "the Himalayas" and for inspiring John Betjeman's *"North Coast Recollections"* and *"Seaside Golf"*. Betjeman is buried in the churchyard at the turn of the course. The club was founded in 1891.

7. Dawlish – another view on a coloured postcard numbered 22106, by unidentified publisher.

6. Dawlish Warren is an unassuming, rather flat links between the sea and the wonderful bird life of the Exe estuary, and is itself a nature reserve. Postcard in the "Dawlish Warren Restaurant Series".

8. Felixstowe Ferry Golf Club (founded 1880). 1910 photograph addressed and written in French to a Mr Massy, in Connaught Square, London: possibly the great French golfer Arnaud Massy, British Open Champion of 1907.

9. Burnham, on a postcard published by prolific West Country firm Montague Cooper, and posted in June 1909. A good view of the scale of dunes through which links courses may play. Note the near 100% presence of headgear in this 1909 scene at Burnham and Berrow Golf Club (founded 1890).

10. Brancaster. Royal West Norfolk Golf Club, founded in 1892, and one of a number of fine links in Norfolk. Described by the sender of this Jacob's photograph in 1927 (J.5661): *"The Golf Links here are on a narrow spit of land which is absolutely cut off from the main land at high tides".*

12. Brora, Sutherland. Club founded 1889. One of the most northerly mainland courses in Britain: an 18-hole course in classic links position. Postcard published by Lilywhite Ltd., Sowerby Bridge.

11. Lossiemouth, home of Moray Golf Club (founded 1889). There are two 18-hole courses here now, but perhaps the hazards are not what they were when this souvenir postcard was bought from James Ross, Stationer, Lossiemouth, judging by the message: *"Lossiemouth is noted for its golf links. Don't you remember reading to me about some gentlemen were playing golf and 3 pounder shells from the warships doing their firing were falling about them. This is the place".* Rub of the green!

13. Kirkwall, Orkney, founded 1889. Even further North! Photographic card in Holmes' Silver City Series, specially printed for D. Spence, Stationer, Kirkwall.

14. Aberdovey, Gwynedd, founded 1892. Superb photographic postcard by George & Son, postally used in March 1913. Aberdovey was the favourite course of Bernard Darwin, the doyen of golf writers, and as such has been much written about. Particularly noted for the hole known as "Cader" with its blind approach and disaster awaiting the inaccurate shot.

Aberdovey Golf Links, The Pulpit.

The Wrench Series, No. 8627

15. Aberdovey – The Pulpit – a well-named tee. Wrench Series postcard no. 8627.

L'ANCRESSE AND GOLF COURSE, GUERNSEY

17. L'Ancresse. Royal Guernsey Golf Club (founded 1890). Aerofilms Photograph 43249 showing the links joining sea to sea.

Llandudno – The Golf Links

16. Llandudno (founded 1894). This card, drawn by Warren Williams in the "Dainty" Series was sent in 1906 to a Miss Grey *"Nr the Primitive Chapel, Motcombe, Sussex"*. Two of the players are wearing red jackets, a form of dress that was uniform for play at some clubs in the 18th century and continued to be used in the 20th e.g. at Bembridge, Blackheath and Chingford.

The Golf Links, Herm.

18. Herm. About as far South in the British Isles as you could go but the course is no more. Postcard by the Guernsey Press Co.

GOLF COURSE, BALLYCASTLE.

19. Ballycastle, Co. Antrim, Northern Ireland. Card published by William Ritchie in the "Reliable" series.

NEWCASTLE FROM GOLF LINKS.
WHERE THE MOUNTAINS OF MOURNE SWEEP DOWN TO THE SEA

20. Royal Co. Down, Newcastle. Valentine's "Phototype" R3034. This is one of a number of great links around the coast of Ireland. Founded in 1889, it obtained a Royal prefix in 1908. Two courses lie at the foot of Slieve Donard, the earlier of which was devised by Old Tom Morris for a £4 fee.

Golf Club House from The Newton Course, Nairn

22. Nairn. Founded 1887. Valentine's Photograph 206154. Note how sand bunkers are a natural feature of links courses; mere holes in the turf, and not artificially built.

GULLANE FROM THE HILL.

21. Gullane. Founded 1882. There are three 18-hole and one 9-hole courses at this club, a stone's throw from the still more famous Muirfield. The No. 1 course is of championship calibre, though rising on a hill above the true linksland. Valentine's 216708.

Old Course and Marine Hotel, North Berwick

23. North Berwick. Note the woman golfer playing back onto the course from the beach. Photographic card by Valentine of Dundee, no. 97085.

THE FIRST TEE, NORTH BERWICK

24. North Berwick. This is one of golf's older (founded 1832) and more hallowed grounds. It originally only had 7 holes. It is first of all a busy, holiday golfing course, but of real quality despite the traffic it carries. Ben Sayers, the famous club-maker was based here; Arthur Balfour, later Prime Minister, was its Captain in 1891. Ritchie's "Twilight" series, posted from North Berwick in August 1910.

25. Rye, Sussèx (founded 1894) on a Frith of Reigate postcard no. 53481. Rye's main claim to fame is that it is the home of the President's Putter. This competition is for members of the Oxford and Cambridge Universities Golf Society who meet every January, often in appalling weather, to play for this trophy which hangs in the club house. It was the putter of Hugh Kirkaldy, Open Champion in 1891. Play is over classic links which, though not the longest in yards, are lengthened by the January weather. Players actually have to carry diagonally the dune ridge featured on the card.

26. Southwold, Suffolk (founded 1884). This Jarrold's series no. 734 postcard illustrates the nature of rough on links courses; low but impenetrable to the clubhead. The message below the picture emphasizes the point: *"I have lost my ball!"*. Card posted to Brighton in August 1902.

27. St Augustine's, Ebbsfleet, Kent (founded 1907 – 18 holes). A delightful sepia photograph. Note the natty clothing. The message reads: *"I like the look of these [links] just as well as St Georges [Sandwich] or Prince's but of course the others both have much more swagger clubhouses!"*.

28. Hunstanton. Near Brancaster, (see above) on the North Norfolk coast, Hunstanton (pronounced Hunston) is a testing 18-hole course; the club was founded in 1890. Photographic postcard no. 60006 by Frith.

CHAMPIONSHIP COURSES

There is no rule that describes an Open Championship Course. But the greatest competitions require courses which provide the greatest test, together with good facilities to allow galleries to see the play and to stay locally. Certain courses have proved to offer these things par excellence, and have thus entered the mythology of the game.

ST. ANDREWS

There can be few cities in the world whose name is synonymous with one specific sport. But mention St Andrews and nine out of ten people will think of golf first, even before the charms of the city or the fame of its University. It was, and is, the home of the world of golf. The first course was here. The game is administered from here.

"The city boasts an old and learned college
Where you'd think the leading industry was Greek;
Even there the favoured instruments of knowledge
Are a driver and a putter and a cleek."

(R.F. Murray 1932)

The lists of local players and Championship winners at St Andrews catalogue the greatest names in the game's past: Tom Morris (Old and Young), "Andra" Kirkaldy, Freddie Tait, the Auchterlonie family; Jamie Anderson, Taylor, Braid and Jones.

The course has been played on for at least five hundred years (and four hundred before the first postcard!). For all of its familiarity the course has baffled even the greatest players. Bobby Jones, who was to become one of its greatest admirers tore up his card in his first attempt in the Open, in 1920. He later called the Old Course *"the most fascinating golf course I have ever played"*.

There are now four courses; a fifth is planned.

29. The Clubhouse, the Royal and Ancient Golf Club. Here is probably the most famous view in golf. Ahead lie the vast area of the first and 18th fairways, the 18th green where so many great prizes have been decided, and the clubhouse which, fine though it is, seems almost unassuming for the position it holds in determining world golf's rules and organisation. Postcard published by Fletcher & Sons of St Andrews.

R. AND A. CLUB HOUSE, ST. ANDREWS.

30. Closer to, it can be seen as a sturdy stone building. The windows on the far side overlook the first tee, making it feel to the humble 'rabbit' paying homage at the altar of golf that the eyes of all golf's 'greats' are watching his first shot – and frowning at the sacrilege. Postcard: Holmes' Real Photo "Herald" series.

31. Cockle Bunker and Strath Bunker, 11th Hole, St Andrews. Throughout the Old Course lies a variety of bunkers which can wreck a round. "Strath", "the Beardies", "Hell", and others can strike terror to the heart of even professionals. "Strath" was named after the 1865 Open Belt winner. It lies in front of the 11th green, which is quite one of the most difficult to 'par' in the world. *"Had round here yesterday, wonderful golfing country, 4 courses. I found this beauty yesterday, its much deeper than shown and well I know it"*, writes the sender of this Valentine's Bromotype postcard in June 1932.

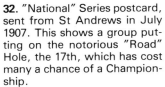

32. "National" Series postcard, sent from St Andrews in July 1907. This shows a group putting on the notorious "Road" Hole, the 17th, which has cost many a chance of a Championship.

THE 18TH GREEN, OLD COURSE, ST. ANDREWS.

33. The 18th. Once past the Road Hole there is "only" the 18th to go. But ... having dealt with the nerves at the start of the round in front of the clubhouse windows, here you are again. *"This one for the Open"*. But straight-forward though the hole is it is too easy to be too far from the hole and to have to avoid a "Doug Sanders". Postcard locally published by the Cathedral Press, St Andrews, and posted from there in July 1925.

34. Prestwick. Although St Andrews has pre-eminence as the home of golf, Prestwick could be called the Home of the Open. Although the event has not been staged there since 1925, when Jim Barnes won, the first twelve Championships, starting from 1860, were all played there. The first, fourth and sixth were won by Willie Park; "Old Tom" won in 1861, 2, 4 and 7; his son in '68, '69, '70 and '72. Andrew Strath was Champion in 1865 to break up the family party. Photographic postcard by Alexander Henderson of Maybole.

Prestwick Golf Course.

At the 9th Hole, Golf Links, Prestwick. 433

35. Prestwick. "At the 9th Hole". Davidsons Real Photographic "Ideal" Series.

36. Royal Troon. On the Ayrshire "Golf Coast" next door to Prestwick, Troon came to Championship prominence with Arthur Havers' victory in 1923. This was the last 'home' win until 1934. Bobby Locke was a winner here in 1950. Another Henderson card, postally used in April 1938.

TROON GOLF-CLUB HOUSE. 301

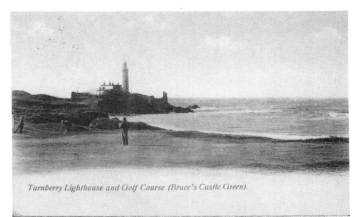

Turnberry Lighthouse and Golf Course (Bruce's Castle Green).

37. Muirfield. Muirfield means two things in the history of golf: one of the very best courses in the world; and the Honourable Company of Edinburgh Golfers. The course is the star turn in a Lothian coastline populated with quality golf: North Berwick, Gullane, Luffness New, Kilspindie, Longniddry and Musselburgh are on the same playbill. But Muirfield stands out. Like on many links courses, you cannot actually see the sea because of the dunes; in fact Muirfield hardly seems like a links course in some respects, lacking their typical wild feel. It is notorious for its bunkers which are many (170 or so) and extremely deep and steep-sided. Early Open winners here have been Harold Hilton (the amateur), Vardon, Braid (twice), Ray, Hagen, Perry and Cotton. Readers may recall the traumatic defeat Jacklin suffered at Trevino's hands in 1972. As to the Honourable Company, this august club in 1764 prepared the rules of golf which were subsequently adopted by the R. & A. at St Andrews and became the official Rules of Golf. The HCEG was based first at Leith, then Musselburgh before making its home at Muirfield in 1891. Postcard: Valentine's Sepiatype series 215609.

38. Turnberry. A few miles south of Troon and Prestwick lies yet another Ayrshire Open venue, Turnberry, with its Ailsa and Arran Courses, famous lighthouse, derelict airfield and splendid view of Ailsa Craig. Its 9th hole is world-famous, demanding a drive from a peninsula tee across both sea and low cliff to safety on a narrow dog-leg fairway. Although only a relative newcomer to the Open roster Turnberry has already seen one of golf's most famous duels; that between Watson and Nicklaus in 1977 which the former won on the 72nd hole despite Nicklaus holing a huge putt. Postcard by Alexander Henderson, Maybole, posted at Maiden in September 1913.

39. Turnberry, the 4th green and hotel. Photographic card by Lilywhite of Sowerby Bridge.

40. Carnoustie. Back to the East coast: Carnoustie is a gruelling, nearly 7000-yard course. The club was founded in 1842 and was a "nursery" for professionals who became the founding fathers of American golf including Macdonald Smith, and Stewart Maiden, the mentor of Bobby Jones. The course features two twisting brooks known as Jockie's Burn and the Barry Burn which easily catch out the unwary. Valentine's Souvenir Postcard 20367.

HOYLAKE, The Golf Club.

Golf Club House, St. Anne's-on-Sea

41. Hoylake. In alternate years the Open is played in England and Scotland, always on links. When in England its home tends to be either in Kent or at one of the great courses close to Liverpool. Hoylake is home of the Royal Liverpool G.C., despite being sited across the Mersey estuary from the city. Other fine courses in the area include Formby, Lytham and Birkdale. In still, dry weather Hoylake seems deceptively easy, but given a wind it takes on a totally different guise. The first course was laid out in a rabbit warren in 1868, and the club house built in 1890. This club produced two of the greatest amateur golfers, John Ball and Harold Hilton, who both won the Open. Ball won the Amateur 8 times as well, and Hilton 4 times. Early Open winners here besides Hilton himself (in 1897) were Herd, Hagen and Jones. Herd's win was the first with a rubber-cored ball, known as the "Haskell". Postcard: Wrench Series No. 458.

42. Royal Lytham St Annes. North of Liverpool, near genteel St Annes on Sea is a course as fierce as any. Lytham St Annes will remain in British golfing lore as the venue of Tony Jacklin's "home" Open win of 1969. It was first chosen to hold the Open in 1926 when Bobby Jones became the first amateur Open Champion this century. Tony Locke won in 1952, Peter Thomson in 1958, Bob Charles in 1963, Gary Player in 1974 and Seve Ballesteros in 1979: the most cosmopolitan list of any Open venue. Postcard from Boots Cash Chemists "Pelham" Series.

Golf Links, Deal

43. Deal. Just as other great links are situated in 'belts' of dunes in various parts of the coastline, so another lies in Kent. Three major golf courses lie between Sandwich and Deal in a continuous Elysian field for the golfer: Royal Cinque Ports, Princes, and St Georges, Sandwich. Of the Cinque Ports course, Deal, Harold Hilton wrote in 1912: *"The links at Deal are perhaps those which approach as nearly as anything in this world ever will the ideal of what a professional deems the perfection of a golf course."* Not only has it hosted the Open twice (Taylor winning 1909 and Duncan in 1920) but it is also the long-standing home of the Halford Hewitt public schools championship. Coloured postcard published by C.W. Faulkner, series no. 522 D.

44. Royal St Georges, Sandwich – lies in the same stretch of links as the Deal course. Founded in 1887, it was a regular Open venue until World War 2, reappearing only in 1981 when American Bill Rogers won; and 1985 when Sandy Lyle of Scotland became the first British champion since 1969. Like Deal, it is also a venue for the Amateur Championship. In 1930 the Walker Cup was won here by the U.S.A. under Bobby Jones, in his Grand Slam year. Fine photographic card by a publisher who gave no indication of name apart from 'H. Bros.'.

45. Sunningdale. Because the Open is always held on links courses, this chapter has so far only dealt with these. Sunningdale is included to remind readers of the quality of inland courses, of which it is one of the finest, and of some of the championships not exclusively played by the sea. It was founded in 1901 among the heather and pines of what would become the Berkshire/Surrey "golf belt", including not only Sunningdale but the Berkshire, Wentworth, West Hill, Worplesdon and others. Ironically, although never able to host the Open, it is famous for the near-perfect Open-qualifying round played there in 1929 by Bobby Jones: 33 out; 33 back; twelve 4s; six 3s; 33 shots; 33 putts. Designed by Willie Park, Ted Ray described it as *"the finest inland course I have ever played over"*. The Ladies Open Amateur; Boys Amateur; Youths Open Amateur; Dunhill Masters; European Open; the Bowmaker; the Daks; the PGA Match Play; the Hennessy Cup; all have been played here. Photographic postcard WHA 5866.

THE GREAT TRIUMVIRATE

46 and 47. These two postcards by Geo. Burley of Skegness show a match between Taylor and Arnaud Massy at Seacroft, Skegness in August 1907. Massy had just become Open Champion at Hoylake, with Taylor runner-up. Head-to-head purse matches between leading professionals were common and popular in those days when there were few tournament prizes available. The Seacroft club was founded in 1895 and still exists.

Controversy will always surround comparisons of greatness between sportsmen of different generations and those concerning golfers are no exception. Was Young Tom Morris better than Vardon? Jones than Nicklaus? What if Freddie Tait had not been killed in the Boer War? How many titles might Cotton have won had not the '39 – '45 War intervened?

Books by the thousand have, largely since the Great War, been published extolling the careers and techniques of this or that hero of the game. Yet in the "postcard era", before 1914, hero-worship was perhaps not quite as prevalent as later. The mass media were not yet hungry for stars on whose names to build circulation. Sportsmen did not yet commonly employ agents to seek out publicity and sponsorship.

So golfing places dominate the opus of the golf postcard era; but the professional game in that same period was dominated by three players who certainly would have gained "superstar" status in later media-dominated decades: the Great Triumvirate of James Braid; J.H. Taylor; and Harry Vardon.

They were born within a few months of one another in 1870/71 but at opposite ends of the British Isles: Braid at Elie, in Fife; Taylor at Northam, in Devon; Vardon in Jersey. The "first to show" was Taylor, who won the Open Championship in 1894 and 1895. Between his first success and the start of the first World War one of the three won the Open on sixteen occasions; and one or another was runner-up on fourteen. In none of these years was one of the three not in the first 2 positions. It is perhaps idle to suggest that any one of them was the greatest, though Vardon won six Opens to five for each of the others.

J.H. Taylor started his golfing career as a boy caddie at Westward Ho! close to his birthplace. When he died at ninety-two years old he was President of the Royal North Devon Golf Club where he had begun all those years before.

He first played professionally in 1891 and in that year was club professional at Burnham. He was seventh in his first Open in 1893 and then began his winning career at Sandwich.

James Braid was born in Earlsferry in Fife in 1870, and died in 1950. He did not come from a golfing family but grew up in a golfing landscape. Though a Scot who learned his golf on links his first professional job was as a clubmaker at the Army & Navy Stores in London. Thence he became club pro. at Romford until 1904 when he moved to the newly opened Walton Heath where he remained for the rest of his days. He was not only one of the greatest players of his day but also a great course designer, being responsible among others for Gleneagles, Blackheath, Nairn and St Enodoc, all of which are illustrated in this book.

48. Photographic postcard showing a match at Budleigh Salterton in 1908. Braid centre, in profile. The card was posted from Budleigh in August that year.

49. Card published by Carlton & Sons, as an advertisement for Woodhall Spa Golf Club. Vardon inset.

Golf Club House, Woodhall

Carlton & Sons, Copyright.

HARRY W. VARDON.

Harry Vardon was, like Braid, born in 1870, in Grouville, Jersey.

As well as having the distinction of the greatest number of Open victories – 6 – (still unbeaten to this day) Vardon probably made the greatest impact of the Triumvirate on the game's future. Vardon's grip, whereby the little finger of the right hand overlaps the index finger of the left, was innovatory. It made the hands work together in a way which had not been common before and which revolutionised ball control. In addition his swing which was much less slashing and more controlled became the model for future generations.

Both the Vardon grip and derivatives of his swing are standard still today. His address and follow-through are shown in this trio of cards.

Vardon was also a course designer, with Royal County Down's 1908 layout and Little Aston to his credit among others.

50. Raphael Tuck "In the Open" Postcard Series 6453 – "Champion Golfers". Posted from London in November 1907.

51. Raphael Tuck "Glosso" Photographic Series No. 1095 "Golf".

GOLF. VARDON DRIVING OFF.

INLAND GOLF

Heath-land

The characteristics of heath-type courses are in the soil (sandy), the vegetation (gorse, heather, bracken and birch), and the relative flatness. They are probably closest to links courses in style, turf and hazard.

The title of this chapter is borrowed from a book by Ted Ray, the 1912 Open Champion, not only because it is the perfect counterpoint to Chapter 1, but because Ray wrote his book specifically to redress the balance of favour of those times from links to inland play.

As the popularity of golf grew, almost every town of any size needed its own course. Indeed, as golf spread across the Atlantic the sheer distances from the coast meant that seaside courses were not within reach of most of the American population.

Golf professionals like James Braid, Willie Park and others were encouraged to turn their talents from play towards course design. Indeed the Great Triumvirate of golf players, Vardon, Braid & Taylor all became inland club pro's.

Many attempts have been made to devise links-type courses inland, some quite successfully. England's first course of all, Blackheath, which was played in 1608, was inland on sandy land somewhat akin to linksland. But the terrain available in most instances precluded this and in time a number of distinctive types of Inland Golf grew up, utilising assets rather than minimising defects.

52. Berkhamsted, Herts., founded 1890. This club shares, with Ashridge G.C., a small pocket of sandy soil atop the chalky Chilterns in West Hertfordshire. The course is tight and deceptively difficult; of sufficient quality to be home to one of the major amateur golf trophies of the year, the Berkhamsted Trophy. Bernard Darwin described it as: *"natural, old-fashioned golf on a Common at its very best"* in 1925. Postcard by Photochrom, Tunbridge Wells, and of late 1930's vintage.

53. Worplesden, founded 1908. Worplesden G.C.'s 18-hole course in Surrey is typical of that area's "sand and pine" terrain which benefits many fine courses nearby, such as Wentworth, the Berkshire, West Hill and Sunningdale. Roger and Joyce Wethered, the brother and sister who dominated English amateur golf between the wars, were based here. This card features the 7th hole.

54. Walton Heath. There are now two 18-hole courses at Walton Heath. The club was founded in 1904, near Tadworth in Surrey. Professional for its first 45 years or so was the great James Braid (q.v.) who in his later years played a "birthday round" in a score of at or below his age. For some reason the player shown on this photograph published by Roberts of Burgh Heath (no. 349) seems to be driving on the green. Note how sand bunkers like those which appear naturally on links are designed into the greensides.

55. Okehampton, founded 1913. Eighteen holes (though originally 9) weave along the very edge of Northern Dartmoor with its *"wonderful moorland turf"* (J.H. Taylor), oak and rowan trees, granite and fast-running streams. Okehampton rejoices in one of the most spectacular of short holes, an 89 yard 12th or "drop hole". The rigours of the geology and climate prevent courses like Okehampton becoming tonsured like lusher areas' courses and enable it to retain a feel of "this is what golf used to be like". Real Photo by Chapman, Dawlish (no. 12971).

56. Bishop Auckland, Co. Durham. An 18-hole course; the club founded in 1893. I hear of high standards of golf here still today, which is probably as well for the local sheep at this lovely hole. Real photographic card by Frith (no. 67152).

Upland

I have linked under this name a variety of types of ecology because, although the vegetation may differ, courses built on hills enjoy common benefits in the very lie of the land. Just as original links used the contours of the sand dunes, courses built on hillsides can similarly use natural geography rather than artificial features to add interest and hazard as well as to enhance drainage.

57. Appleby, founded 1903. More daunting still than Bishop Auckland's or Okehampton's ruggedness is this view of Appleby G.C. in Cumbria. There appears to be nothing which could be called a fairway for these players to aim for, in this postcard from J. Whitehead & Son, posted from Appleby in May 1909.

Gleneagles Hotel—The Tinkler's Gill Green.

58. Gleneagles, Perthshire. The very antithesis of the rough-hewn, basic charm of some uplands courses is represented by the haute couture of Gleneagles' courses, as exampled by this publicity card for the Gleneagles Hotel. The use of the terrain is, however, classic, in this James Braid-designed course.

GOLF CLUB HOUSE, PITLOCHRY.

59. Pitlochry. Not far from Gleneagles, and still in Perthshire, is Pitlochry, where the delightful if literally breathtaking first three holes lead uphill to wonderful views and splendid use of the contours. Card by Valentine of Dundee, postally used in August 1935.

First Tee, Braid Hills Golf Course, Edinburgh

60. Braid Hills, Edinburgh (founded 1893-4). Coloured photographic postcard by M. Ware & Co., Edinburgh. This is the course *"which more people play over than play over any other course in the world"* – E. Ray 1912. The card was posted from Edinburgh in February 1907.

GOLF COURSE, STRATHPEFFER.

62. Royston G.C., Herts. Chalk downs perhaps make the most attractive hillside golf courses. Close-cropped turf; natural curved lines; good drainage and somehow more than their share of skylarks all contribute. Royston was founded on Therfield Heath in 1893 and is the author's current home club. In between it has been the favourite course of John Maynard Keynes and Leonard Woolf. Postcard published by Robert H. Clark: 85 Royston, "The One Hill", and posted from there in July 1911.

85. Royston, "The One Hill".   Robert H. Clark's Series.

THE DOWNS & GOLF HOUSE, WARMINSTER.

63. Warminster (founded 1891). This 1913 photographic postcard shows the contrast between farmland terrain and that on the chalk hill.

EASTBOURNE, PARADISE DRIVE AND GOLF LINKS.

64. Royal Eastbourne G.C. This club celebrated its centenary in 1987. The featured "Paradise Drive" was a "favourite" run for boys of Eastbourne College, who had to run the gauntlet of flying golf balls where the course crosses the road. Photographic card postmarked 1913.

61. Strathpeffer Spa, Ross & Cromarty. An 18-hole course, formed in 1888. Postcard by Valentine in their "Sepiatype" series 79017 – addressed to Major Gen. Sir S. Hill-Chind CB. KCMG. DSO, Club of Western India, Poona, India in 1922 – must have made him homesick!

"Parkland" as a description of inland courses tends to mean that the course was built in cultivable land often near towns. It often also infers lush grass and broadleaved trees; sculpted bunkers in inconvenient places and high, stopping shots rather than low runners.

66. Lamberhurst G.C. In the Weald, Lamberhurst is typical, pleasant parkland. Now 18-holes, the club started with a 9-hole layout in 1892 and is thinly disguised as Siegfried Sassoon's Amblehurst in *"Memoirs of a Fox-Hunting Man"*: *"a hazardless nine-hole course round Squire Maundle's sheep-nibbled park"*. Card published by the R.A.F. Co. Ltd.

65. R.A.C. Country Club — Woodcote Park (founded 1913). This club is said to have the largest membership in the world. It has two 18-hole courses near Epsom in Surrey, a convenient distance from central London for an afternoon's golf. Real photograph.

67. Exeter Golf Club (founded 1895). This 1920's photographic postcard seems to sum up the golf of that time: stylish! But the view is of typical parkland layout.

68. Fulwell. An 18-hole course founded in 1904 to the West of London in a now increasingly built-up area. Note that the description "Links" is still used, though erroneous. This photographic card clearly shows one of parkland's attractions: the blossom on the trees lining the fairway.

69. Wigan G.C. A 9-hole course established in 1898. Note the use of the twee name — this hole is called "Dirty Dick" — one of the less endearing golfing traditions borrowed from the Scots by English clubs. Card by Cyril Foley, Wigan.

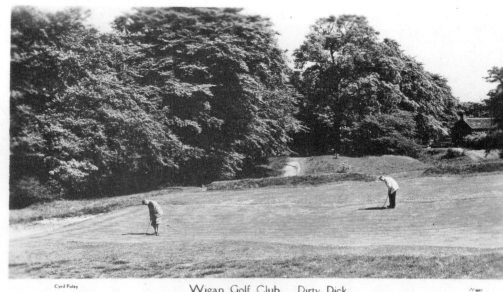

Wigan Golf Club. Dirty Dick.

Hall Garth Links, Hornsea.

70. Hornsea G.C., Hall Garth Links, Yorkshire (founded 1908). Photograph by Thos. C. Wise.

71. Invertilt Golf Course, Blair Atholl. This course is very flat, on parkland in front of Blair Atholl Castle. The bunker ridge in the foreground typifies the artificiality of hazards in parkland courses. Valentine postcard no. 202207.

202207 J.V.   Invertilt Golf Course, Blair Atholl

NINETEENTH HOLES

*"Is not yon club house, looming near
A home of hospitable cheer?"*

It is easy to forget sometimes that golf courses and golf clubs are not the same thing. Club and course go together because in the main their existence is interdependent. As far as we can tell the course was the first on the scene, among those famous dunes on the Fife coast. But the history of golf owes as much to the Clubs which formed the Rules; to which players belonged; and which provided clubhouses.

In these, members could meet, form policy, change clothes, refresh themselves, declaim absurd feats, and do all those other things related or unrelated to golf which makes the game more than just striking a ball round a course.

Clubhouses reflect the diversity of courses: from forbidding to lowly; from pretentious to rustic.

72. Moor Park G.C. Next door to each other, with courses and character quite different from one another just outside London are the Moor Park and Rickmansworth Golf Clubs. Their club houses shown here reflect the very essence of golf's variety and attraction. No two courses, or clubs, are the same. Moor Park G.C. is housed in this magnificent mansion, once the home of Lord Ebury. The club was founded in 1923 and occupied the house 14 years later. There are two 18-hole courses there now. This postcard (AGC Series 131048) dates from 1918, before the club existed.

73. Rickmansworth G.C.'s home on the other hand has other charms. In fact the course is a public one; short but with lovely turf. This photographic postcard is by R. Miller of Rickmansworth and postmarked 1910.

74. Shandon. Further down the scale of opulence still, but I am sure no less loved by its occupants, was Shandon G.C.'s home in Belfast, founded in 1926. Postcard: "Reliable" Series 827/45.

-26-

75. Shrub Hill, Chesterfield, Kent, proclaimed on some postcards as "the oldest club house in the country". But it wasn't purpose-built as a club-house. The club, founded in 1925, occupies what was an ancient manor and its barn. Postcard by West & Son, Whitstable.

76. Eltham. Today the home of Eltham Warren Golf Club, this fine Adam house in 1923 also became the home of Royal Blackheath G.C., the oldest club in England, when it was forced to abandon its original eponymous site because its wear by golfers and public had eroded it beyond use. The course is described in the Badminton Golf (1895) as *"rather flat ... It is umbrageous golf and in the right season the nightingales sing cheerily in the hedges".* Postcard by G. Rathbone, postmarked 1905.

77. Royal Ashdown Forest G.C. A club that has its home right in the middle of the course, which boasts no artificial hazards. Postcard by Photochrom, postmarked 1904.

78. West Essex G.C. Chingford. This club was formed in 1900 with this custom-designed building typical of its day. The course was designed by James Braid. Photograph by A. Pettit, Chingford.

79. St Anne's Old Links G.C. (founded 1901). This famous club, in the Lancashire golfing belt, has an imposing home, shown on this Valentine's postcard no. 7106, dated 1912.

80. Cromer. The age of the golf boom, in the late Victorian period, was heavily influenced by the styles and experiences of the Empire, particularly to the East. Bungalows with verandas, such as were enjoyed in the foothills of the Himalayas, lent themselves to the needs of golf clubs, and many were built for this purpose. Royal Cromer G.C. was formed in 1888. This postcard is postmarked 1910.

81. Porthcawl. The late Victorian club house of the Royal Porthcawl G.C. in Glamorgan. The course overlooks the Bristol Channel, which can be seen from every hole. Founded 1891. Postcard published by Comley & Son, Cardiff, Series 315, and posted at Porthcawl in September 1904.

82. Wimbledon Park G.C. was founded in 1889. The postcard is from J.H. Blakes "Idler's Own" series of local views, no. 103.

83. Little Aston G.C. at Streetly, Staffordshire, which opened in 1908 with a course by Braid. Photograph by D. Darby, Streetly, no. 187-15.

84. Selsey. A typical clubhouse of its day: this belonged to Selsey G.C., founded in 1906 with a nine-hole layout. Photograph by M. Gardner, Selsey, no. 216, postmarked 1914 from Chichester.

85. Ballantrae. Even some much less well-endowed clubs adopted the style of the "Far Pavilion". Alas Ballantrae is no longer with us, though in 1927 it had a healthy 200 members.

86. Killiney, Co. Dublin. The "Empire" style reached Ireland, too, in those days, as shown in this postcard by Hely's Ltd. of Dublin, sent in 1906 when the clubhouse was only three years old. The message reads: *"Driving a tremendous ball! Open stance with a magnificent finish. This is a splendid clubhouse 3 times as big as Tavistock"* to Mr. E. Metters, Golf House, Tavistock.

87. Greystones. Another Irish clubhouse is shown on this attractive touristy Valentine's postcard no. 51593. The club, in Co. Wicklow, was founded in 1895.

RHÔS-ON-SEA GOLF CLUB, Colwyn Bay. TEL No. 48.
Club House on the Electric Tram connecting Colwyn Bay with Llandudno.   Always open to Visitors.

89. Rhos-on-Sea (founded 1899). This advertisement for the club rightly features the clubhouse as a major attraction. The card was sent from Colwyn Bay in August 1915.

90. Woodhall Spa (founded 1905). Another Hotel for golf, just to emphasise the scale and affluence of the game in the past. The 1928 sender says *"got my car cleaned and polished for me this morning by a chauffeur of a R.R. that is putting up in same place. He said he'd so much time on his hands he'd be thankful for the job".* Postcard by Heale.

91. Kingsdown. Clubhouses may offer, in addition to the requisite facilities for members, the bonus of position. This photographic postcard shows Walmer and Kingsdown G.C. (founded 1909) sitting on the very end of the White Cliffs of Dover, looking North-East over the Channel.

92. Sunningdale. Photograph by WHA no. 1659. Perhaps the epitome of English inland golf courses, Sunningdale rejoices in a classic club house. For comment see "Championship Courses".

93. Goodwood G.C. We started this chapter with the grand and so we shall end it. Goodwood has an 18-hole course founded in 1892. The clubhouse style is quite unique.

(opposite page)

88. Portrush. This is not the clubhouse, but the Golf Hotel built for this famous course. Founded in 1888 to make use of some wonderful linksland for golf, the Royal Portrush G.C. is the only club outside mainland Britain to have hosted the Open (in 1951 when Max Faulkner won). Sandy Herd was professional here, and there are now two 18-hole and one 9-hole courses. William Ritchie's "Reliable" series postcard no. 754/136.

HAZARDS OF GOLF

Into each life some rain must fall but as if that were not enough golfers must also cope with bunkers and other hazards placed in their errant way by either nature or course designers. Even early golfers had this cross to bear; bunkers originate in the sand scrapes around rabbit holes, further eroded by weather and sheep, sheltering from it.

When golfers moved inland its architects "invented" the bunker again; but a new sculpted version, carefully placed to catch the unwary or unskilled.

At the greenside, modern professionals are said to prefer to have to hole in 2 from a bunker than from the rough. The average club golfer is usually glad just to escape.

When it comes to some of the monsters shown here, even professionals of past times with the equipment of the day may have felt that way too.

*"An even temper strive to keep
When trapped in hazards wild and deep."*

94. Gigha Bunker, Machrihanish, 1919. This scale of bunker is only to be found on links courses. Machrihanish is at Campbelltown, Argyll & Bute. The course was designed by Old Tom Morris of St Andrews and opened in 1876. *"The glories of the links of Machrihanish are sung by all who have been so far afield to visit them."* said Horace Hutchinson in the Badminton Library. Postcard published by A. Livingstone, the Store, Machrihanish.

95. Leven. This Valentine's Series postcard of Leven Links was from the days before the sand wedge, whose heavy and shaped heel drives it through sand and helps bunker play. Perhaps the golfer's companions shown are watching to see the technique needed to play a sandshot with a blade club. Leven is one of the older Scottish courses, having been founded in 1846.

96. Colonsay. How about this for a daunting start to a round? The card was published by the local Scalasaig Hotel, whose ideas on attracting golfing visitors were somewhat unusual. Though only 4775 yards long, with hazards like this is doubtless no pushover.

97. Alnmouth. An early Northumbrian club, founded in 1869, shown in this 1926 photographic postcard. The first bunker here shows how deep bunkers in sandy terrain often had their faces shored up with sleepers.

98. Brancaster. Another sleepered bunker is shown in this Jacobs photographic postcard (J7223). It is addressed from a mother to her son at Marlborough College: *"This is the sort of thing I have been struggling in"*.

99. Sandy Lodge. This club, near Northwood in Middlesex, occupies a rare sandy pocket in an area otherwise devoid of sand: *"As you may suppose, sand bunkers everywhere"*. The card is dated 1914 when the club was only four years old. Note the piles of sand ready to create new horrors! Most inland courses lack indigenous sand and must both create the hazard and fill it.

100. Stanmore (founded 1893). Quite close to Sandy Lodge lies Stanmore. This club is older but not blessed by the sandy soil so, like many inland courses, had to resort to artificial mounds like these shown in 1908, when the card was posted.

Golfing—A Difficult Shot

101. Golfing – A Difficult Shot. Not all hazards are sandy. Grass bunkers hold their own terrors but water is uniquely difficult to play out of because of the refraction. Postcard from Valentine's Series "Golfing", and published in 1902.

102. Littlehampton Links – Flooded March 1915. J. White of Littlehampton photographed this scene and published the result, no doubt much against the Committee's wishes had they known. Not so much a hazard as a disaster: sea water can do near-irreparable damage to grass.

On Tain Golf Course

103. On Tain Golf Course (founded 1890). Many more rural courses allow sheep to graze on the fairways, even when play is going on. This keeps the grass under control and simultaneously "feeds" it, though the resultant lies may leave something to be desired! Davidsons Real Photographic Series.

GOLFING HUMOUR

There must be more jokes and tall stories about golf than about any other sport. This is reflected in the huge number of humorous postcards published both early this century and since. Some of the great illustrators turned their hands to this new genre, as can be seen in this chapter. Golf jargon lends itself to puns ("spooning", "playing the game", "playing a round" etc.). It is also worth noting the frequent appearances of caddies in these postcards. These are perhaps testimony to their reputation for dry comment on their temporary employers' standards of play; but also to the important position they held in the game. They were not merely bag carriers but experts in local knowledge who could win or lose a match for their employers by their advice – and commentators on the absurd. *"His anecdotes, autobiographical and local, which at first amuse, become intolerable as the match closes in darker and darker at each hole"* said Sir Walter Simpson, the 19th century golf chronicler.

104. Tom Browne was one of the best known of postcard and book illustrators of the turn of the century who used golf as a regular subject. "Spooning by Moonlight" was published by Davidson Bros., as were most of Browne's cards. This is from series 2640.

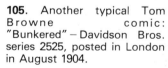

105. Another typical Tom Browne comic: "Bunkered" – Davidson Bros. series 2525, posted in London in August 1904.

Golfing Jokes from *"Punch"*. A series published as postcards by Raphael Tuck in the *"Oilette"* series 9142.

106. *"Aunt Jubisca"*. Drawn by A.T. Smith.

107. *"Jones has told me …"*. Drawn D. Wilson, posted at Callington in August 1906.

108. *"Carry your caddy, sir?"* Drawn by O.D. Armour, and sent from Norwich to Holt in February 1906.

Cynicus was both artist and publisher of illustrated humorous postcards. His earlier ones were produced at Tayport, Fife, the later ones at Leeds. These cards are from a set of six featuring golfing vicars.

109. *"Not lost but gone before"*, with Port Erin overprint and postmark of 15 August 1907.

110. *"Two up & one to play"*.

Reg Carter was at his peak between the world wars. In these two examples of his golfing cards he stereotypes beautifully men's golfing dress of the day: tweedy plus-fours, loud checks etc.

GOLFING TERMS ILLUSTRATED:—
TWO DOWN—AND ONE TO PLAY.

112. *"Driving all over the place"* – overprinted "at Kelly Bray". E.T.W. Dennis & Sons, London & Scarborough. Mid-1920's vintage.

JUST A FEW WORDS

113. Brian White cartoon (published by Valentine in their 'Nipper' series no. 3511) showing the frustrations of the game. Once in the trap the object is to get out. Efforts are not always rewarded with success! Card posted at Huddersfield in August 1937.

111. *"Golfing Terms Illustrated: Two up and One to Play"* (note the frequent use of his golfing score as a pun). "National" Series postcard no. 3500. Postmarked 1932 from Birmingham.

114. "A Stopped Ball! Oh!" Cartoon by 'Bob', published by Felix Rosentiel, and posted at Bradford in October 1904. Another example of period golfing attire.

115. *"You never shouted 'fore'"*. William Ritchie "Reliable" Series No. 9362 features a cartoon by G.F. Christie, posted at Evercreech in August 1908.

116. *"They ca' me "Breeks" but my maiden name's McIntosh"*. Published by Millar and Lang of Glasgow & London in their "National" series. Postmarked 1908, from Margate. The artist was 'A.A.'.

117. "The Rules of Golf". What more serious golfing topic can there be than the rules? Therefore it was natural that a series of humorous satires on them should be published. In fact Perrier, the French mineral water company, sponsored this famous series drawn by Charles Crombie. This example, from the "Golf Series" G431, was posted at Stockwell in November 1907.

118. Phil May's famous postcard design *"I miss you awfully"* in Raphael Tuck's "Write Away" Series 1008.

119. The Game of Golf – one of a series of six "Golf" postcards by Raphael Tuck. *"Your Honour"* is no. 743 and shows the relationship between caddie and player in early days: the upper-class golfer towers over the diminutive and no doubt poor caddie. Yet somehow we know who will get the best of the verbal encounter. This was an early (about 1901) comic postcard.

120. This humorous card drawn by 'Mart' for E.T.W. Dennis may caricature the way golf dress "progressed" (?) with the years but by today's gaudy standards even these fine fellows may look drab. This is from the 1950's.

121. Mabel Lucie Attwell. A surprise subject for this famous children's illustrator, perhaps. Valentine's postcard 2830 from the 1930's.

122. *"Am I On It Caddie?"* Bamforth published this golfing version of the funny fat lady in their 'Comic' series no. 2025.

123. The standards of illustration and humour have by no means improved as the comic golfing postcard has been updated. For the sake of propriety some even more "modern" postcards have been omitted! Design by Trow from the early 1960's – card published by C. Richter of London N.W.6.

STYLE

"Style" means many things: fashion; elegance; method. In golf, as in most things, style has changed with the times. Fashion has always been particular in golf whether illustrated by the suited-and-tied early professionals; the red coats of early amateurs; the tweedy plus-fours of the "clubbables" or the multicoloured casual wear of todays jet-setters.

Elegance may best be seen perhaps in the manners of golfers through the ages: Freddie Tait; Bobby Jones and Gene Sarazen were exemplary.

And as to methods: well, there are about as many as there are golfers.

However, despite the diversity of styles which postcards have depicted, some examples catch the character of earlier days.

Golf Links by the Sea, Bexhill-on-Sea.

124. Bexhill-on-Sea. This lovely 1912 sepia photograph from Barker's Library at Bexhill has it all: the fashion of the day, elegance and a very period golf swing. It was once regarded as unseemly for women to swing the club above elbow height; and in such long dresses might have been quite a feat anyway.

125. This German golfing party at Bad Wildungen, Brunnenellee (by F. Schubert) also shows the typical dress of the first decade of the century for golf: high collars; hats; buttoned jackets; long skirts.

126. Golfing: Driving Off. An example of the early "bent left elbow technique" which Vardon's style superceded. Even the caddies wear jacket and tie. Valentine series postcard, postally used from Mayfield, Sussex, on 29 November 1903.

(handwritten) 29/11/03. Don't you wish you could join them in a game? N. S.

Golfing.—Driving off

127. Golf: Bunkered. A good photographic illustration of both player and opponents in this Tuck "Glosso" postcard (series no. 1095. "Golf"). The player's stance is "open" and he is playing out sideways from the bunker. Without the sand wedge it was difficult to cut the ball up quickly enough to play straight over such a steep face. N.B. The player is wearing a left-hand glove, which was less common then than now.

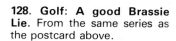

GOLF. BUNKERED.

128. Golf: A good Brassie Lie. From the same series as the postcard above.

GOLF. A GOOD BRASSIE LIE.

"His Master's Handicap."

129. "His Masters Handicap". Caddies too had style – of a kind! But nothing to match the elegantly spatted shoe of His Master! Henderson "Golf" Postcard Series B9 no. 2596. Cartoon by Chas Crombie.

130. Golf: Putting. Here is a good juxtaposition of styles in 1905, drawn by G.D. Rowlandson for C.W. Faulkner & Co. Series 372E. Casual elegance and smart dress for the players and their two children but a less assured demeanour for the caddies. The wide stance for putting was more common in those days than now.

Golf: Putting.

ADDRESSING THE BALL.

131. "Addressing the Ball". It was not surprising if some caddies learned precocious style, as Lawson Wood illustrated for Tuck's *Oilette Connoisseur* postcard no. 2930 sent in 1914 from Cricklewood.

WOMENS' GOLF

The custom in golf is to refer to female players as "Ladies". There is, however, something both prim and elitist about this word so this book at least refers to them as women.

Women's golf is definably different from mens'. Physical limitations are compensated by greater suppleness which in today's women's game makes for swings often far closer to the ideal than those of leading men.

But consider how long the freedom to benefit from this elasticity was constrained both by convention and by clothing. Women's golf is as old as we can trace the game. We have pictorial evidence of Stuart princesses playing. As a competitive sport, though, it is younger than the male game, the first championship being played in 1893, between thirteen entrants. Mrs Gordon Robertson was the first woman professional in 1905. Yet by 1912 there were four hundred and nine women's clubs affiliated to the LGU and the game was flourishing at home and overseas.

"Women as a rule, play the game more economically than men. They do not take caddies so frequently, and when away for a golfing holiday they content themselves with humble lodgings, whilst the "superior" sex goes to the hotel. Women's clubs too are run on a cheaper scale than men's clubs," stated the New Book of Golf in that year.

Women in early days sometimes had not only their own clubs but also their own courses, including one at St Andrews, shown here. The Ladies Putting Club was founded in 1867. Often these were little more than putting greens, or pitch and putt courses because of the limited distances early women golfers could hit the ball. But as the decades fell away so did the inhibitions of convention and fashion, and women more frequently shared the larger courses.

132. On the Ladies Golf Course, St. Andrews. A postcard in the 'Royal and Ancient Series' by W.C. Henderson & Son, St. Andrews, posted from there in September 1908.

133. The Golf Girl. E.J. Hey published this postcard of a Cecil Quinnell painting. It carries a 1918 National War Bond postmark.

134. Cruden Bay G.C. was founded in 1791 at Port Errol, moving to the current location in 1899. How did early women golfers manage to enjoy even the walk, let alone the game dressed this way: full-length dress, wide-brimmed hat and all? It was here that, in 1919, Mrs Alan MacBeth was the first woman to compete in an open tournament. Postcard published for Wm. Bremner, Chemist, Port Errol.

135. Machrihanish (see "Hazards of Golf", illus. 94). But manage they did, as this Valentine's series no. 34715 shows, though these women belie the introduction's stereotype by all having caddies, in 1907: "jolly good links", says the sender.

136. Golf, On the Green. A good close-up of pre-first world war golf garb. Tuck "Glosso" series 1095.

GOLF. ON THE GREEN.

137. Abersoch, North Wales. The woman golfer 'in action' has a shorter skirt but her companion's is still full in length. The follow-through is typically low compared with those of today. May's Photo postcard series, retailed by Roberts' Stores, the Post Office, Abersoch, which offered *"the largest selection in North Wales".*

138. Valentine's Series — Golf. Such round-armed strokes could result in disaster for both caddie and spectator! Note the illustrated footwear's heels — and on sand at that.

139. Llandudno. Here is evidence of a woman or girl acting as caddie on Llandudno Links, whose club was formed in 1894. Postcard by Pictorial Stationery Co., London.

LLANDUDNO. The Golf Links.

140. Seaford Head G.C. (founded 1907). By 1915 skirts have risen to just below the knee: hats are still worn. Postcard: R A Series, posted at Seaford in April 1915.

141. Ashdown Forest. Many Ladies Clubs had their own clubhouses, as here. Frith & Co. No. 59997, with August 1909 postal usage.

142. and here, at Lundin Links. Postcard published by P. Scott, Largo.

143. West Cornwall (Lelant) 1930. A similar length of skirt to that of 1915. Friths Postcard Series Real Photo: for Frank Lake, St Ives.

144. West Lancs. Ladies G.C. This very early photographic postcard shows the nature of the Ladies course at Blundellsands to be pretty testing.

GOLF. THE LADIES TEE.

145. Royal Cromer G.C. used Ladies' tees, as most courses do now. Tucks "Glosso" series 1095.

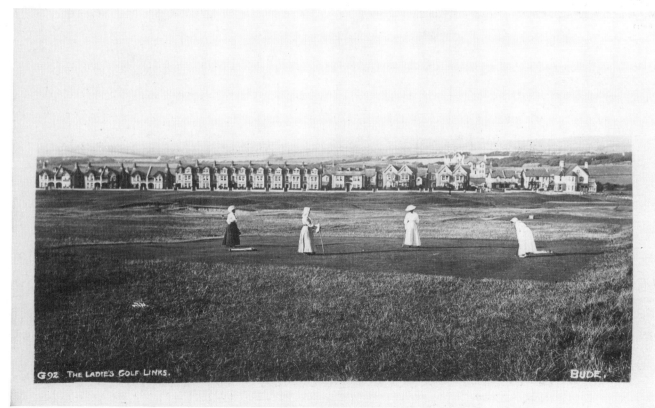

G 92 THE LADIES GOLF LINKS.   BUDE.

146. Bude *(see 'Holiday Golf').* If you met these four out shopping I bet the last thing you'd think they were planning was a round of golf!

HOLIDAY GOLF

One of the greatest attributes of golf is that it can be enjoyed at every level. Other chapters have called to mind some of the names and feats of the great professionals and top amateurs of the past. But golf is much more than a game for the expert. Even the high handicapper can derive huge enjoyment from golf. The half dozen or so good shots in a round of nearly a hundred can produce a rosy glow even without the help of the "nineteenth hole", whilst the sheer pleasure of playing a relaxing game in the fresh air in lovely surroundings takes some beating. Hence the success of the game as a participatory, rather than merely a spectator sport, both now and in the past.

It was no accident that so many resort towns attracted golf clubs; nor that resorts grew around golf courses favoured by views, good weather and railway connections. Golfing holidays are no new phenomenon either at home or abroad. Indeed to some degree they were more popular in days past when golf was more of a family game.

The West Country; the Ayrshire coast; Norfolk's seaside towns and many other places blossomed as golfing holiday resorts.

Inland, too, the space of the Highlands, of Ashdown Forest and other unspoiled areas lent itself to course building and to holiday-making for golfers.

The popularity of golf as a holiday pastime is reflected in the preponderance of postcards from such resorts in the early part of this century.

147. Newquay. The illustrator Robert Carline in 1906 captured the joys of holiday golf on this postcard advertising the Headland Hotel at Newquay. This sums up all that is good in holiday golf. The course dates from 1890; the card was posted from the resort in July 1913.

Mullion Golf Links.

148. Mullion. Constructed five years later than Newquay, Mullion is similarly beautiful in outlook but shorter, being less than 6000 yards long. It lies on the Lizard and is the most southerly mainland course in Britain. A.A. Milne, of Winnie the Pooh fame, played here and wrote his poem *"The First Tee"* about Mullion:
*"Down to the sea the close-cropped pastures roll,
Couches behind yon sandy hill the goal".*
Postcard: Friths Series No. 64019.

149. St Enodoc. Close to Rock, Padstow, Trebetheric and Polzeath, St Enodoc serves as a focal point for holidaymakers in North Cornwall. It is a links course celebrated for its huge "Himalayas" bunker and by its late resident poet Laureate, John Betjeman. Founded in 1890 with a layout by James Braid.

NATURE'S OWN INSPIRATION!

Nature, with the unintentional assistance of Man, designed this portrait of Colonel Bogey, Trevose, and evidently intended that here, of all places, his heart should be wrapped up in golf. The coast line and roads are correct with the map, the Colonel's left eye is exactly in the position of the Coast Guard Station and his right eye would correspond to the Trevose Lighthouse, which is near the cliff edge on the far side.

150. Trevose Country Club. Still today a major golfing holiday centre, Trevose advertised itself as such in a unique way on this postcard. Though only a short distance as the golfball flies from St Enodoc, the two courses are separated by an estuary. It was designed by the famous golf architect H.S. Colt and opened in 1924, with entrance fee and subscription each of 2 guineas.

Golf House, Bude

151. Bude and North Cornwall G.C. Bude has attracted golfers as well as holidaymakers ever since it opened its club in 1891. The course and the clubhouse come right to the edge of both town and beach, where its lovely turf must be a magnet to golfers on their way to surf. Postcard in Voaders Series, postmarked April 1921.

THE GOLF LINKS
BUDLEIGH SALTERTON

152. Budleigh Salterton's cliffs have been home to the East Devon G.C. since 1902, offering this view to the East towards Dorset. A.R. Quinton illustrated it for this Salmon Series postcard no. 3274.

GOLF LINKS THURLESTONE

153. Thurlestone. The children on the beach; parents on the tee: a perfect holiday for all. This principle makes Thurlestone a popular golf resort to this day. It was founded in 1897. Photographic postcard by "Ruth".

154. Freshwater Bay, Isle of Wight. A little further to the East and just as attractive, it seems.

The Golf Links, Freshwater Bay, I.W.

COODEN BEACH GOLF LINKS. 5.

155. Cooden Beach. Further eastwards still lies Cooden near Bexhill in Sussex. A rather flat but deceptively difficult seaside course, built in 1912.

156. Royal Cromer. Another famous stretch of holiday golf which should not be neglected for the siren lure of the Algarve lies on the Norfolk coast between Hunstanton to the West and Mundesley to the East. Royal Cromer, shown on two postcards pre-and-post dating the building of the clubhouse, was founded in 1897 with a 9-hole course. Part of this disappeared by cliff erosion and the current 18-hole course wisely shelters behind the lighthouse. Salmon Series "Sepia" Style – note the bathers walking up the path.

157. Another view of the same course. Valentine's Series Souvenir Postcard 23989.

158. Sheringham (founded 1891). Just to the west of Cromer lies Sheringham with its much-postcarded golf course, similar in type to Cromer and very popular in the early part of this century. Postcard in B.A. Watts Series, postmarked 1908.

159. Scarborough. No prizes for guessing how this holiday is to be spent! Scarborough has two clubs now: the North Cliff and South Cliff. But when this postcard was sent in July 1905 only the 1903-founded South Cliff existed. Postcard illustrated by "C.M.C." and printed by Tomes of Leamington.

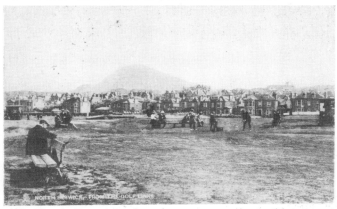

160. North Berwick. A major resort on the Lothian coast, North Berwick is a championship course among championship neighbours like Gullane and Muirfield. Postcard in Tuck's "Sepia" series no. 2403, sent from North Berwick on Christmas Eve 1909.

161. Aberdour, Fife. It must be hard to keep the eye on the ball at this hole. The view is of Bell House Rock and Ingholm Monastery with part of Aberdour G.C. (founded 1904). Postcard: Tuck *"Oilette"* published specially for Donald McLaren, Stationer and Fancy Goods Merchant, Aberdour.

162. Harlech, Gwynedd. Harlech is the home of one of the most popular of golf clubs, the Royal St Davids, founded in 1894. The then Prince of Wales was Captain in 1935, giving cause for the "Royal" prefix. In one direction, behind the clubhouse, towers Harlech Castle, as on this Valentine's Photographic Postcard W2420.

163. In the other direction from Harlech clubhouse stretches the view towards Snowdonia (Frith's Series No. 85647).

164. Abersoch. Also in Gwynedd is this club founded in 1907. This panoramic photograph by Valentine shows its attractions.

> Having rapidly circumnavigated the mainland we should not omit to sample the opportunities for a holiday inland. These examples may whet the appetite.

165. Gleneagles. The capital of inland holiday golf, with its vast hotel and four courses, Gleneagles offers perhaps the finest scenery for a golf course simply because it was put there to do so. James Braid and Major Hutchinson designed the first course, the Kings, opened in 1919. Its invented names for its holes lack something in spontaneity. Familiar to millions from televised pro-celebrity games. Valentine's Photograph A8991.

166. Cleeve Hill, Cheltenham. The Cotswolds' beauty and the architectural charms of Cheltenham make a holiday in the area highly worthwhile, the more so when golf played on a course with views like this can be added. Postcard: A.R. Quinton illustration for Salmon postcard no. 1445.

167. Crowborough. Another Quinton Watercolour (Salmon 1369). Crowborough Beacon G.C. lies on the edge of Ashdown Forest in Sussex, home of Winnie the Pooh; a natural ancient heath with lovely views. Sir Arthur Conan Doyle was a member of this club, founded in 1895.

168. Cromer. The last postcard in this chapter enables a link between holiday golf and the top professionals to be forged. This relaxed pair are doubtless admiring the poppies and the view as they enjoy a holiday game, following the advice of the great Walter Hagen that the game be not taken too seriously and that golfers *"be sure to smell the flowers along the way"*. Parsons Norman is the artist on this postcard published by Jarrolds of Norwich and posted on 2 April 1914.

FOREIGN FAIRWAYS

As Scotland's game spread to the South in the late nineteenth century, so it travelled abroad in the cabin trunks of its newfound converts. First across the Channel; then the servants of the Empire took it to the Eastern colonies; at length emigrants, particularly from Scotland, introduced golf to the USA, which in too few years was to come to dominate the sport.

Although countries far and near continue to learn to like golf, it was in the decades either side of the turn of the century that the foundations were laid for what became a global game.

Within Europe, the number of clubs founded before 1900 was small, but the names of their locations betray the roots of their foundations, British diplomacy and leisure:

Biarritz. Berlin. Dieppe. Cannes. Wiesbaden. The Hague. Opporto. Malta. Las Palmas. Engadine. Gothenberg. Copenhagen.

And to keep in touch with home in those pre-telephone, pre-airmail days, what better than postcards?

346   LE TOUQUET-PARIS-PLAGE. — Le Golf, son nouveau parcours — LL.

169. We start our Grand Tour close at hand across the Channel at Le Touquet. *"Le golf son nouveau parcours"* says this 1910 postcard of the then brand-new course at the popular society resort. There are now two 18-hole and one 9-hole courses. Postcard by Levy et Neurdein of Paris, posted from Le Touquet in September 1910.

170. Another Le Touquet scene, this time published by A. Hourdier — it shows the newness well; but later Horace Hutchinson was to call Le Touquet *"the best seaside golf in France"*.

171. Hardelot. Not far from Le Touquet was the course at Hardelot. *"Un des meilleurs Golf-Links en Europe"* claims the advertising copy on the reverse. But would-be visitors looking for golf may have been put off by the daunting tee shot facing this young man. Postcard by Valentines.

Hotel du Golf par Etaples 8 th Green

172. Etaples. 8th Green, shown in 1909.

153 VITTEL   Terrasse du Golf (Fernaud César, arch., Nancy)

173. Vittel. Elegance seems the by-word in this stylish clubhouse at Vittel. The postcard even refers to the architect (Fernaud Cesar of Nancy). Postcard by CAP (Compagnie des Arts Photomecanique) of Strasbourg.

(9680) ARCACHON
Golf et Country Club, angles des Boulevards Deganne et Mestrezat.
Près du but.
HENRY GUILLIER, 31, 42 bis et 44, rue Fonneuve.   LA COTE D'ARGENT

174. Arcachon. The "society" side of golf is well shown on this postcard by Henry Guillier but look at the handicap carried by the lady putting!

175. Pen-Guen, Brittany. A most attractive postcard map of the course at the course taken from Dinard. Postcard by E. Imbert & Cic, Grasse.

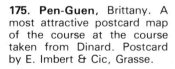

GOLF DE PEN-GUEN

176. Monte Carlo. "Le Golf du Mont-Agel" illustrated on this postcard by Robaudy of Cannes. Course described as *"possibly the most breathtaking in Europe"*.

177. Knocke Le Zoute, Belgium. Advertisement for the resort published by A. & G. Bulers, Brussels, featuring golf.

178. Further afield, Nuwara Eliya golf club in Ceylon, now Sri Lanka, looks a golfing paradise. Participants wore tropical kit, solar topees and all. The Green fee was 3 rupees per day in 1927. Postcard by Platé & Co., Ceylon.

179. Mombasa, Kenya. Postcard published by Tokin Productions (*The Times,* Mombasa). Note the "brown" (green) made smooth for putting by spraying oil on the sand. 9 holes.

180. Bulawayo. It *says* it is the Golf Links but where to drop the ball? "Sapsco" Real Photo, Johannesburg.

181. Royal Calcutta G.C. "Empire builder" shorts help in hot climates. The clubhouse could as easily be in Surrey! It needed to be big; thee were 1600 members in 1927. Postcard by C.F. Hooper, Calcutta.

182. Hong Kong. The course at Fan Ling, Hong Kong lies both inside and outside the race course. Message on this postcard, published by O.F. Ribeiro, states – in 1904 – *"Not such a good links as our Westward Ho!"* Indeed not.

183. Hongkew Park, Shanghai. At last! Some locals, as opposed to Europeans, playing. The tee looks well trodden too.

And so to the U.S.A.: a small sample of postcards to represent the huge growth of the golf there.

184. Lenox Valley and Golf Links, Lenox, Massachusetts. "Phostint" Card, Detroit Publishing Co.

187. Catalina Island, California, on a card published by Adolph Selige and posted in Los Angeles, July 1907.

185. Beardsley Park, Bridgeport, Connecticut. Published by 'C.T.' of Chicago.

188. And finally, Pebble Beach, on the Monterey penninsular, in California. One of the best courses in the world still today. Hand-coloured postcard by the Albertype Co. Brooklyn, New York.

186. Druid Hills Club, Atlanta, Georgia, on a card published by I.F. Co. Inc., Atlanta.

VANISHING GREENS

Golfers who are also travellers may be heard to mutter to themselves as they view an appetising but course-less landscape *"If only ..."*. How much more *"if only"* could be overheard were they to realise how many fine courses which once existed are no more.

In 1911 J.H. Taylor could list some 750 English courses. Although now there are over 1,200, there have been many casualties on the way. In one county, Devon, there was no increase in courses in the seventy years after JH's list. Ashburton, Chagford (Meldon), Bolberry, Prince Hall, Woolacombe, Lee, Totnes and Dartmouth have all gone.

The reasons for this are as diverse as the uses to which good land may be put but housing and military needs have been regular culprits. Whatever the "cause of death" this chapter commemorates just a sample of what we are missing, in memory of all the others.

189. St Margarets-at-Cliffe, Kent. On the White Cliffs of Dover, this course had disappeared by 1947, presumably unable to survive the war. It had an 18-hole course, offering special terms for "Naval and Military Officers on Active List". Photographic postcard postmarked 1909, published by J.B. Madge, Post Office, St Margarets-at-Cliffe.

190. Norbury. This attractive club had disappeared by 1927, which is all the sadder because of the dearth of golf courses in the heavily built-up areas of South London. Photographic postcard from the "Anchor" series, published by the Photo Printing and Publishing Co., Croydon.

191. Street, Somerset. Presumably the course lies on the hill behind the pine trees, where it must have provided splendid views. Card postmarked 1928, from the "Alice Pile" series, Street.

192. Woolacombe. One of the many courses to have disappeared from Devon, as mentioned in the introduction to this sad chapter. Like nearby Saunton *(see illus. 1)* this course was used by United States troops in the Second World War for training, but alas, unlike Saunton, was not restored. It was an 18-hole, links course, where, as at many clubs in past times, no Sunday play was allowed. The record score for a competition round in Britain, 55, was scored here in 1936. Postcard advertising the Woolacombe Bay Hotel, by Norman Bros., Cheltenham.

193. Portishead, Nr Bristol. An 18-hole course overlooking the Bristol Channel. Postcard by Valentine for Bowen's series, Portishead, postally used in August 1909.

194. Tintagel. What a wonderful place for a golf course. The club was called the King Arthur's Castle G.C. (Phone No: Tintagel 2!). A 9-hole course. Photograph by Ronald Youlton of Tintagel.

195. Chagford. High on Meldon hill overlooking the Dartmoor town of Chagford lay, until disuse allowed bracken too strong a foothold, a 9-hole course. The club in 1927 had but 30 members. The depression, together with the logistical problems of reaching Chagford by public transport, may have contributed to the loss. Real Photographic postcard by Chapman & Son of Dawlish, no. 10065. *(Jane Somers Cocks collection)*

196. Bolberry. Another clifftop site now course-less, this time in South Devon. It became an airfield, but not before being snapped for posterity on this W.R. Gay photographic postcard.

197. Raynes Park. An early club in the way of London's expansion, no doubt. Sandy Herd won a tournament here in 1896. Postcard published by the Collectors' Publishing Co., London E.C., and posted in May 1905.

198. Alexandra G.C., Westcliff-on-Sea. An impressive facade shown on this coloured postcard of 1906, in the 'A.J.H.' series.

199. Manchester G.C. This rare card shows the original site of Manchester Golf Club (founded 1882) which moved from Trafford Hall to Hopwood in the late 1890's. The card is postmarked, notwithstanding this, in 1908. Vardon won here in 1898. Published by Whittaker & Co., Gaff series no. P216.

TRAFFORD HALL, TRAFFORD PARK.

GOLF LINKS & BEACON HILL, TOWYN.

200. Towyn, Merionethshire. A real loss by the look of this postcard. It was an 18-hole course which survived the second world war. Photographic postcard by Robert J. Williams, Towyn, posted from there in September 1915.

Greenock. From Golf Course.

201. Greenock. The club, designed by James Braid, was founded in 1890 overlooking the Clyde and the town. It survived until quite recent times.

GOLF LINKS AND BEMBRIDGE FROM ST. HELENS. I.W.

202. Bembridge, Isle of Wight. The Royal Isle of Wight G.C. was founded in 1882 and had been described as *"one of the best 9-hole courses in the world"* – and *"very good and sporty"* by H. Hutchinson – yet survives no more. Photographic card by Dean, Sandown, in the "Bay" series.

The Golf Course, Kippford.   269/151

203. Kippford, Kircud-brightshire, a 9-hole course which has disappeared since 1945.

204. Wemyss Castle G.C., Fife, on a postcard by Valentine.

WEMYSS BAY FROM GOLF COURSE.   B.6395.

No.1 TEE. GOLF LINKS CHISELDON.

205. Chiseldon. This was the attractive site of Swindon G.C.'s original home. Fortunately the club still thrives, down the road at Ogbourne St Georges. Photographic postcard by Hooper, Swindon.

Postcard Publishers

Wherever possible within this book, the caption indicates the publisher of each card. Such were the vagaries of postcard publishers, however, that in many instances there is just no indication of which firm or individual was responsible for a particular card.

Postcards, particularly before the First World War, were produced on a series of different levels. Locally, in almost every town in the British Isles, there existed firms — often just a simple individual — who would produce cards in small quantities, depicting local events and views. While some of these publishers were extremely professional in their approach, others produced cards anonymously, sometimes with crude, handwritten captions.

At the next stage were 'area' publishers, who covered one or more counties — examples in this book include the Devon firm Chapman of Dawlish, who produced a fine record of West Country photographic cards over a period spanning half a century, and Norwich publishers Jarrold, who sold both viewcards and artist-drawn cards.

Then there were the larger national firms whose output of postcards covered the British Isles, and in the case of the biggest — Raphael Tuck and Sons — the world. This London-based company published cards of all types, and their golfing output included views of courses, comic cards and special photographic series (see illus. 127, 128 and 136 for three excellent examples). Other top firms who aimed to provide a wide coverage included Valentine of Dundee, Salmon of Sevenoaks (specialists in water-colour scenes by famous artists like Alfred Quinton and C. Essenhigh Corke), and William Ritchie of Edinburgh.

Cards by these national firms were often issued in sets of six, sometimes with a series title. Because they published in far greater quantities than local concerns, cards by Tuck, Valentine and so on are generally much easier to find. Some publishers like the Rotary Photographic Co. Ltd specialised in personalities of the day rather than viewcards. Others, such as the Tayport firm of Cynicus, published almost exclusively comic cards.

The following list summarises some of Britain's top publishers of the pre-1939 period, examples of whose work appears in this book:

J. Beagles, London
Chapman & Son, Dawlish
Cynicus Publishing Co., Tayport
Davidson Brothers, London
E.T.W. Dennis, Scarborough
C.W. Faulkner, London
F. Frith, Reigate
Jarrold & Sons, Norwich
Lilywhite, Halifax
Millar & Lang, Glasgow
Photocrom, Tunbridge Wells
Pictorial Stationery Co., London
Rapid Photo Printing Co., London
William Ritchie & Sons, Edinburgh
Rotary Photographic Co., London
J. Salmon, Sevenoaks
Raphael Tuck & Sons, London
Valentine & Sons, Dundee
E. Wrench, London

GETTING IN ON THE ACT

As we have already seen, the heydays of golf and the postcard coincided. So too did the careers of various music hall, theatrical and film "stars" who were only too glad to use the coincidence as part of their publicity.

208. Lily Elsie, Edwardian actress. The postcard, by Rotary Photo, London, announces *"This is a Hand-Painted Real Photograph of a British Beauty"*. It might also have added *"and on a real golf course."* too! Most such pin-up shots were done in the studio but Stanmore G.C. plays host here.

206. Miss Nina Sevening. Slightly embossed photographic postcard of this actress, who was much "postcarded". Published by the Rapid Photo Printing Co., and postmarked Boscombe, 1908.

209. Miss Kathleen Vincent by Rotary Photo: another "British Beauty", postmarked Sidmouth 1915.

207. Vilma Banky, on a card by Barton Pictorial Co.

210. Mr. George Alexander. The men got in on the act as well. Rotary Photo Book-Mark card 9701b. Every inch the golfer of the times – note the boots.

211. HRH The Prince of Wales. It was not only film stars who were subjects of public admiration, though film star good looks help, of course. Even the highest in the land have allowed themselves to appear on the acceptable medium of the picture postcard. (His father, after all, is on the stamp). The Prince of Wales, later King Edward VIII was, however, a genuine and keen golfer. Beagles Postcards 327U, posted at Hastings in August 1927.

212. Ronald Reagan. Of course some of the highest in some lands *were* film stars *and* liked publicity ... *"All-round athlete Ronald Reagan demonstrates good form on the golf course"*. Postcard published in 1980 by Coral-Lee of Cordora, California, U.S.A. Photo by Michael Evans.

213. Biarritz. VIPs treated certain continental resorts almost as part of the British Social Scene and as such introduced golf to many areas. Here Lord Dudley, Viceroy of Ireland (hard to imagine it now, isn't it) is seen chatting to Mr. Balfour (Arthur Balfour, Prime Minister and golfer) in 1908. Postcard published by Eugene Pacault of Biarritz.

PUBLICITY AND ADVERTISING

Mass advertising was not the feature of life in the early part of the century that it is today. There were relatively few media available: the picture postcard was one.

Towns seeking tourist trade, hotels and golf clubs seeking visitors, and manufacturers promoting products all used picture postcards.

Generally, the advertising element was subsidiary to the illustration.

215. The Dunlop Junior. A testimonial advertisement showing the professional C.H. Mayo apparently using the product whilst on his winning ways. Published by Dunlop Rubber Co. Ltd., Birmingham. Photo by "Sport and General".

214. Bexhill-on-Sea. Humorous postcard illustrated by J.L. Biggar, customised for Bexhill-on-Sea. Published by E.T.W. Dennis & Sons Ltd., London & Scarborough, and posted from Bexhill in September 1930.

216. A Quiet Game at Bournemouth. Well-known illustrator Lance Thackeray is used to promote Bournemouth on this Raphael Tuck *"Oilette Remarque"* Postcard 9305 in the "Game of Golf" series 2. Sent on Christmas Eve, but postmarked Christmas Day 1909!

217. Chick Golf Balls. The North British Rubber Co. Ltd. published this "Elcock"- illustrated humorous card in a series on the Etiquette of Golf. The back lists the brands of the manufacturer: "Chick". "Big Chick". "Clincher". "Diamond Chick". "New Hawk" and "Osprey" Golf Balls. Postmarked 1924, from Cheltenham.

218. The Rosslare Hotel. Illustration by 'Jotter' (Hayward Young); this hotel advertisement features golf by means of an inset. Sent as a Valentine's Day greeting in 1913.

219. Gleneagles Hotel. Gleneagles golf courses are described elsewhere. This attractive Tuck postcard shows both the golf and the purpose-built hotel off to perfection. The back features an advert for the owners, the London Midland & Scottish Railway.

220. Dexter Right Hand. An advertising card for the Dexter Rubber Core Ball published by the manufacturer, the Argus Golf Ball and Requisites Manufacturing Co. This is a double, unfolding card with a lengthy panegyric about the product inside.

Charles Dana Gibson, American illustrator of the famous "Gibson Girls" who regularly lured postcard golfers from "keeping their heads down", drew these golf scenes amongst his extensive repertoire.

221. *"Golf Term. Two up and the ..... to pay"* no. 893 from the "Humorous" series 127 of James Hendersons "Sepia" series postcards.

222. *"Is a caddie always necessary?"* Postmarked Wellington (Shropshire) in October 1908.

223. *"The Ancient and Honourable Game"* "Gibson" series no. 149 by the same publisher.